THE JAPANESE SPIDER CRAB

Table of Contents

The Japanese Spider Crab 2
Getting to Know the Japanese Spider Crab 3
Behavior 13
Habitat 14
Diet 15
Life Cycle 16
Fishery 24
Threats 26
Life Span 27
Japanese Spider Crabs and Humans 28
Disclaimer 30

PUBLISHED BY:

Tanya Turner
Copyright © 2018

All rights reserved.

No part of this publication may be copied, reproduced in any format, by any means, electronic or otherwise, without prior consent from the copyright owner and publisher of this book.

The Japanese Spider Crab

Have you seen a crab that has such long legs that it looks like a spider? Meet the Japanese Spider Crab!

This unique looking crab is quite scary – not only because of its looks, but because of its size, too. This is one dinner that won't fit into your plate.

As deceiving as its appearance may be, know that it's still a crab – classified as a crustacean, just like any other crab.

Like the spider, it also belongs to the order of Arthropods (which also includes scorpions and lobsters). The Japanese Spider Crab holds the record for being the Arthropod with the largest leg span.

In spite of being scary-looking, this sea animal is said to be a gentle creature. Would you dare to stand face to face with it?

Getting to Know the Japanese Spider Crab

It's really quite easy to recognize the Japanese Spider Crab. Just think of it as a VERY big crab with REALLY long legs. Its main body can measure up to 16 inches and its leg span can measure up to 12 feet from one tip of a leg to the tip of another leg. A Japanese Spider Crab this big can weigh about 42 pounds. Yes, a really big Japanese Spider Crab can be bigger than a man, and its size makes it capable of eating small animals.

The color of Japanese Spider Crabs also makes them different from other crabs. They have orangey shells and their legs are also colored orange with some white spots.

Note, too, that there are some differences between male and female Japanese Spider Crabs. For one, the female's abdomens are wider than that of the males, but slightly smaller. The female's claws or pincers are also smaller than the males.

It's also important to know that this animal's shell has a rough, bumpy surface. It works as the crab's camouflage as it looks like the rocky ocean floor. As its camouflage, predators that are hunting for live food to eat won't easily see the Japanese Spider Crab. It also works in catching live prey for food as small animals can swim by the crab without realizing that it's there. This crab sometimes even allows sponges and small animals to live on its shell as it helps in hiding them better.

Keep in mind that as adults, the size of the Japanese Spider Crab's shell remains at the same size throughout its life. As a young crab, their shells do start out as small – but these grow in size as they mature. But once they are officially adults, the growth will stop. It's not the same with their legs, however.

As the most noticeable characteristic of the Japanese Spider Crab, it's interesting to note that their legs keep growing longer and longer as they age. That's the reason why really old Japanese Spider Crabs can also have really long legs.

They use most of their legs for walking and climbing onto rocks at the bottom of the ocean. To make this task easier and simpler for them, the tips of their legs curve inwards to help them maintain their balance on the sea floor. Having legs with curved tips also helps them to hold onto rocks when climbing so that they won't slip.

Every once in a while, you will see Japanese Spider Crabs with missing legs. This is quite normal, as they sometimes need to defend themselves from their enemies. And so, they can get injured when they get into a really serious fight.

Losing a leg or 2 is actually a good thing if they can escape with their lives, right? Besides, they can lose up to about 3 legs and still live a normal life under the water. Their legs will grow back anyway, although it will take some time. So, while they still have some missing legs, they will not be able to defend themselves as effectively as when they have a complete set of legs.

The scariest part of the Japanese Spider Crab is their claws. Can you imagine being pinched by those big pincers? Or worse, can you imagine being attacked by a Japanese Spider Crab with open claws? That would be a nightmare!

Their pincers are really scary and it's just right to avoid being nipped by their claws. These are huge and strong – and because of their body composition, they can extend their claws and reach out when attacking something (or someone).

Think about it, small crabs (those that are usually served as food) have claws that can injure a person. Can you imagine the damage that the claws of a Japanese Spider Crab can do?

Fortunately, Japanese Spider Crabs are not like spiders that are normally found at people's homes. They are not even present in forests – so you surely won't encounter one when you go camping. They live in the deep sea, where it's dark and isolated from humans. Human encounters with these sea creatures are therefore limited, not unless you intentionally search for them in the deep waters.

Behavior

According to some explorers that have dived into the deep waters to meet some Japanese Spider Crabs, this animal is quite nice. Well, nice in the sense that they don't attack people.

Still, some divers have also reported being attacked by these sea creatures – so that can be quite scary. Remember that even nice animals can attack people when they feel threatened, so one should still be careful when faced with animals that can really cause some serious injury (don't forget their big, sharp claws!).

Habitat

Japanese Spider Crabs can be found in the seas of Japan and Taiwan. While young crabs mostly stay in shallow waters, the adults can be found in deep waters (up to about 1,970 feet below sea level).

True to the nature of crabs, Japanese Spider Crabs also like staying in holes and caves that are found in the deep. They can also stay on the ocean floor while camouflaged with algae and sea creatures.

They do have a preference in water temperature. They can be mostly found in waters with temperatures of 50 to 55 degrees Fahrenheit. While this is the ideal water temperature for them, they can also tolerate water temperatures that range from 43 to 61 degrees Fahrenheit.

Diet

Japanese Spider Crabs are omnivorous animals, so they eat both meat and plants. There are lots of aquatic plants, seaweeds and algae under the sea, so they can eat those as food. They can also capture and eat small animals (remember, this crab is very big).

As scavengers, they don't even look for fresh (and live) food to eat. They can eat dead animals that they find in the sea and ocean floor.

Life Cycle

The months from January to April are the mating season for Japanese Spider Crabs. During this time, the males and females will mate with one another.

Unlike other egg-laying sea animals that lay their eggs on the sea floor or on rocks or on the leaves of aquatic plants, Japanese Spider Crabs don't just leave their eggs anywhere.

Like other species of crabs, the Japanese Spider Crab also carries its eggs on its underside. The female crab takes care of all her eggs until they hatch and become larvae forms of crabs.

Japanese Spider Crabs lay A LOT of eggs per breeding season – about 1.5 million eggs. Yes, that's a lot, and you would think that this will cause an overpopulation of the species – but that's not really the case. Sadly, only a few of the 1.5 million eggs will survive because they will be exposed to a lot of predators in their larvae form (when they stay in shallow waters).

Each egg will measure about 0.63 to 0.85 millimeters in diameter, which is small (and almost microscopic). Well, if the eggs were any bigger, the female Japanese Spider Crab will find it hard to carry all 1.5 million eggs near her abdomen, right?

The development of the eggs can take about 54 to 59 days, after which, they will hatch in about 10 days. And at this point, the female Japanese Spider Crab needs to expose her eggs to a temperature range of about 54 to 59 degrees Fahrenheit. This is the ideal temperature for the crab's developing eggs.

At its larvae stage, the Japanese Spider Crab will take on the form of small rounded sea animals. They will have transparent bodies – and at this point, they will be legless for a while.

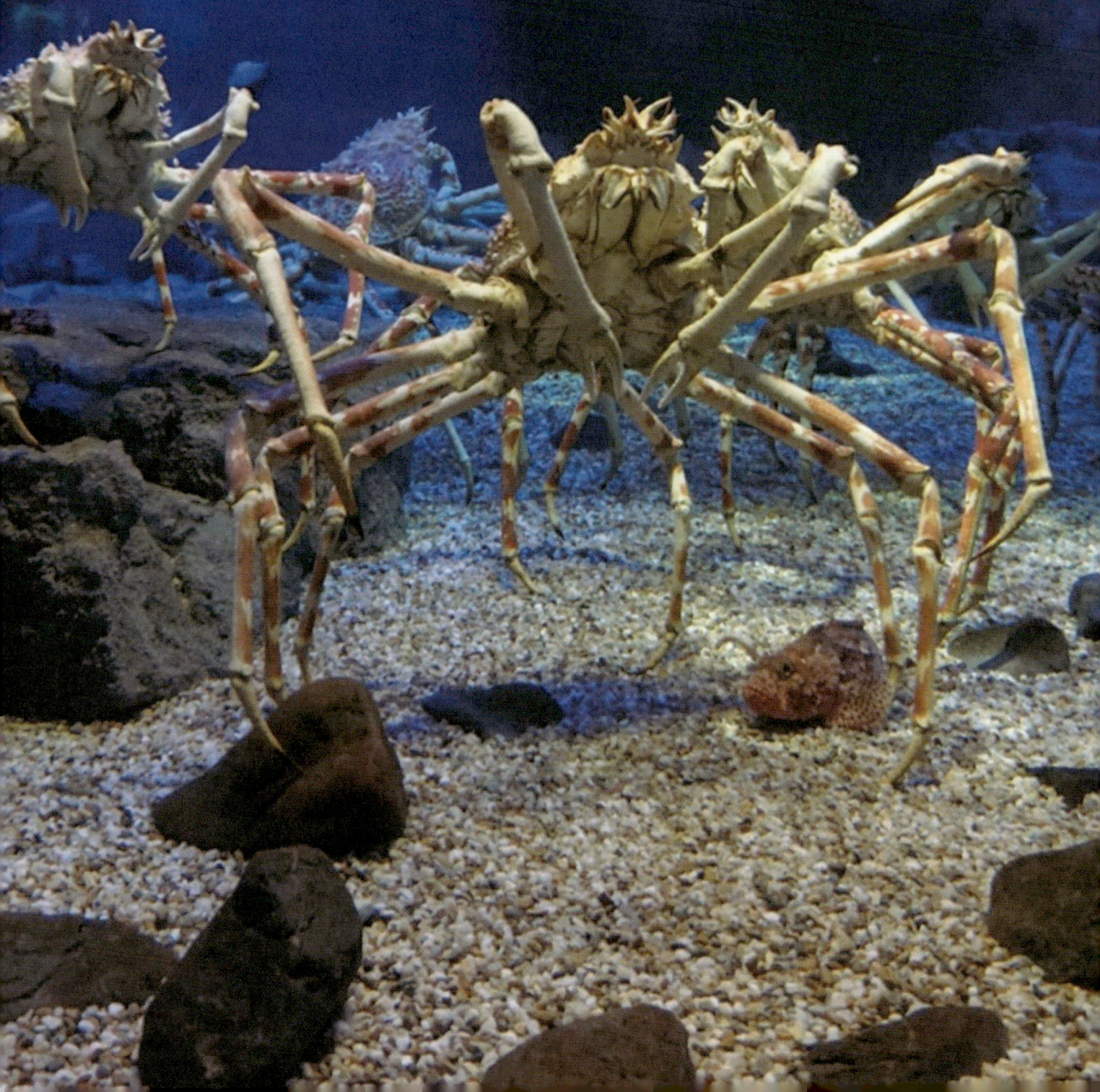

As larvae, Japanese Spider Crabs will also float on shallow waters – very much different from the adults that stay deep in the water. This is actually one of the reasons why only a few Japanese Spider Crab larvae survive as there are lots of predators near the surface of the water.

Once the Japanese Spider Crab larvae have completed their metamorphosis or transformation from larvae to little crabs, they will break free from their enclosure. This is like a plastic covering, and the little crabs will wriggle and twist their way out of it. Since they already have claws, the little crabs will pull the covering off themselves to be free.

As a young crab, the Japanese Spider Crab will slowly mature into adulthood. Its body and shell will start to grow and its legs will become longer and longer as it ages.

Fishery

Although it's not very easy to catch Japanese Spider Crabs because of their size and claws, they can still be caught in nets and traps. For such sea creatures as crabs and lobsters, trawling nets are used as these can scrape through the bottom of the ocean floor and catch these types of sea creatures.

The Japanese Spider Crab is actually a popular dish in Japan. So popular in fact, that harvesting them has become very frequent. And because of this, people are forced to go to deeper waters for more supply.

In order to maintain a healthy population, however, people are not allowed to harvest Japanese Spider Crabs during spring time. You see, this is the time of the year when this species of crab goes to shallow parts of the sea to breed and reproduce. So, by catching them, they won't have a chance to lay their eggs and increase the population of their species.

Threats

As the Japanese Spider Crab lives in deep waters, there are very few species of animals that are there with them. This works well for the crab as big sea creatures are particularly few where they live, so their predators are limited as well.

And if, indeed, there are other sea animals that decide to prey on the Japanese Spider Crab, they will think twice about it as this crab is big and scary-looking. Not to mention its capability to defend itself with its big, strong claws!

Life Span

The Japanese Spider Crab can live up to about 100 years. Yes, that's pretty long. And to think that their legs keep on growing and growing as they age, you can already tell why there are some Japanese Spider Crabs that are really so big.

Just think about it – they can even outlive people, as very few people can reach the age of 100.

Japanese Spider Crabs and Humans

Japanese Spider Crabs are said to be delicious. So, if men can catch them, men will eat them.

There's really nothing wrong with eating such types of animals as food. People have been eating crabs (usually the small types) for many years.

The only thing that people should be concerned about, really, is the Japanese Spider Crab's population. We certainly don't want them to become extinct as that would mean the end of them. What people can do, then, is to allow these sea creatures to breed and multiply so that more Japanese Spider Crabs will live in the ocean.

Disclaimer

The information contained in this ebook is for general information purposes only. The information is provided by the authors and while we endeavor to keep the information up to date and correct, we make no representations or warranties of any kind, express or implied, about the completeness, accuracy, reliability, suitability or availability with respect to the ebook or the information, products, services, or related graphics contained in the ebook for any purpose. Any reliance you place on such information is therefore strictly at your own risk.

Images Credit
Images produced under creative commons licensces are duly attributed.

H. Zell/Commons.Wikimedia.org
Laika /Commons.Wikimedia.org
Trance Light/Commons.Wikimedia.org
Takashi /Commons.Wikimedia.org
Sean Pavone/Shutterstock.com
Andrey Armyagov/Shutterstock.com
Bildagentur Zoonar GmbH/Shutterstock
TDway/Shutterstock.com
Goodboypic/Shutterstock.com
Thanachit Krikeerati/Shutterstock.com
f11photo/Shutterstock.com
zuttinee/Shutterstock.com

James/Flickr.com
Takashi /Commons.Wikimedia.org
Trance Light/Commons.Wikimedia.org
H. Zell/Commons.Wikimedia.org
Momotarou2012/Commons.Wikimedia.org
Tsarli/Commons.Wikimedia.org
Takashi Hososhima/Commons.Wikimedia.org
Laika ac/Commons.Wikimedia.org
Teddy Yoshida/Commons.Wikimedia.org
pelican/Commons.Wikimedia.org
Chris Gladis/Commons.Wikimedia.org
Stefano Stabile/Commons.Wikimedia.org
American Museum of Natural History
/Commons.Wikimedia.org

Printed in Great Britain
by Amazon